DAVID PORTEOUS ART AND CRAFT BOOKS

Flower Painting Paul Riley
Intimate Landscapes Paul Riley
The Dough Book Tone Bergli Joner
Fun Dough Brenda Porteous
Paperworks Dette Kim
Wooden Toys Ingvar Nielson
Papier Mâché Lone Halse
Pressed Flowers Pamela Le Bailly
Silhouettes in Cross Stitch Julie Hasler
Cats: A Cross Stitch Alphabet Julie Hasler
Gift Boxes Claus Zimba Dalby
Decorative Boxes Susanne Kløjgård
Paper Craft Dette Kim
Fairytale Doughcraft Anne Skødt

Gift Boxes

CLAUS ZIMBA DALBY

DAVID PORTEOUS
CHUDLEIGH · DEVON

A CIP catalogue record for this book is available from the British Library

ISBN 1 870586 18 2

Published by David Porteous
PO Box 5
Chudleigh
Newton Abbot
Devon TQ13 0YZ

Copyright © 1991 Forlaget Klematis

Danish edition © 1991 Forlaget Klematis: Gave-Bogen

English edition © 1994 David Porteous

Translated by Tim Bowler

Printed in Singapore

CONTENTS

INTRODUCTION

This book is about boxes and various types of packaging. The first sections show how you can wrap gifts, including bottles, in smart, attractive ways and how you can make some beautiful bows. Often, what really gives the perfect finishing touch to a parcel is a wonderfully large and decorative bow, and you'll find lots of ideas in this book.

Japan is very well known for its beautiful gift-wrapping paper and exquisitely wrapped parcels, and it is customary in that country to offer a gift, and to receive one back, whenever you visit anyone. These gifts need not be expensive or large – small objects are quite sufficient – and the art of folding boxes made from card or paper to contain these tokens derives from Japan. France too is renowned for its attractive packaging. If you go into a store that specializes in chocolates, for example, you will find dozens of pretty boxes, in all shapes and sizes, in which your selection can be packed.

The rest of this book, therefore, includes lots of different boxes that you can make from paper and card. Use them for gifts large and small and to show the recipient how special you think they are.

As you will see, there is not a great deal of text on the pages that follow. Instead, you will find illustrations throughout that make the steps involved easy to follow. Next to the heading for each item is a number in brackets; the number indicates the page on which you will find a colour photograph of the item.

You will also notice that each project title is followed by one, two or three little boxes. These indicate the level of difficulty of each one – one box means that the item could be made by children from about the age of nine years; two boxes mean that it could be made by children from about the age of eleven years; and three boxes mean that it could be made by nimble-fingered youngsters from about the age of thirteen upwards.

Have fun!

Claus Zimba Dalby

MATERIALS

Paper

There are many different kinds of gift-wrapping paper available. In general, it is best to use sheets of wrapping paper because these are more robust than paper sold in rolls. The paper has to be strong enough to be folded and bent back without tearing or coming apart as you work.

So that your package is always perfectly finished off, you must make sure that the colours you select enhance each other – for example, any bows or ribbons you use must match or complement the paper. You should also consider the gift itself and the intended recipient. Should the wrapping be smart and sophisticated or colourful and flamboyant?

If you want to use gift-wrapping paper to make a box, you can stick it on to card that is a matching colour. Make sure that the card is not too heavy (see page 11). When you fold the box, the usual method is to arrange the paper so that it forms a pattern on the outside of the box, but you can also create an attractive effect by having the patterned paper on the inside.

When you glue the paper to the card, use either a glue stick or a spray adhesive. The disadvantages of spray adhesive are that you must never inhale the fumes and the spray itself can raise a lot of dust. If you do decide to use spray adhesive, work outdoors whenever you can or at least make sure that your workroom is thoroughly ventilated.

You must apply an even coat of adhesive to the paper and make sure you do not miss any spots. If you do, the paper may come loose in places when you cut or trim it to size.

You can also use less traditional materials for packaging – old newspaper or corrugated cardboard, for instance – or you could even decorate paper yourself, by printing, painting or drawing your own designs on it.

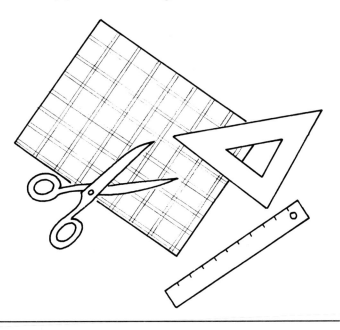

Card

Most of the boxes in this book are made from folded card. Most stationers and shops that stock artists' materials will have a wide range for you to choose from.

It is important that you use the correct weight. If the card is too light and thin, it will not keep its shape. At the same time, it should not be too heavy and thick, because it might break when you try to fold it. A weight of 150–180gsm (56–67lb) is adequate for very small boxes, while you will need card of 190–220gsm (70–82lb) for the larger ones. The best way, however, is to experiment with different weights until you find one you are happy with.

Finally, different cards have different finishes. Some are perfectly smooth, almost glossy, while others have a rough texture and may have a somewhat pitted surface. The choice is yours.

Bows and Ribbons

Often it is the bow and ribbon that give the perfect finishing touch to a present. Stationers, craft shops and the haberdashery departments of most large stores stock a wonderful range of ribbons in different colours and widths, some matt, some shiny, and you must choose a shade and finish that perfectly match the colour of the paper or card you have used for the box.

For large bows you need a ribbon that will remain quite stiff when it is tied, and it is usually better to use one of the synthetic materials than silk or satin. You can buy rolls of synthetic ribbon in different widths and colours, and they have the great advantage that you can make them curl by pulling them over the blade of a pair of scissors or a knife.

If you buy silk ribbon, which is available in some very pretty colours and several widths, you should iron it lightly on the wrong side or under a damp cloth to smooth out any odd creases before you use it.

Needlecraft and haberdashery shops usually have a range of satin ribbons, which, because they are usually slightly shiny, can look very smart and sophisticated. The narrowest widths are ideal for small boxes. Haberdashery shops often also stock all kinds of exciting materials that you can use – zigzag braid, lace or velvet ribbons, for example.

Finally, if you feel that a more rustic finish is appropriate, you could use paper ribbon, raffia or even twine.

TOOLS

You must have the correct tools ready before you begin. There is nothing more infuriating than having to stop halfway through a project to search for something you need. You will use some or all of the following equipment for the boxes in this book.

Adhesive tape Use adhesive tape where it will not be visible. The most useful kind is double-sided, which is, in any case, essential when you are wrapping presents and making bows.

Carbon paper You will use carbon paper to transfer a drawing or template from one piece of paper or card to another. Never transfer a design directly from the book. Draw the template on to tracing paper or photocopy it, then place a sheet of carbon paper on the paper or card, place the tracing or copy over the carbon paper and go over the outline with a pencil. Enlarge the template as necessary on a photocopier or use the grid method (see page 14).

Compasses Use a pair of compasses when you want perfect circles.

Craft knife A craft knife is often easier to use than a pair of scissors. The best and cheapest are the kinds in which the blade is located within the body of the knife and sections are snapped off as they wear down. You could also use a scalpel. Remember that both tools can be dangerous and must always be used with care.

Darning needle Use a large darning needle or blunt-ended tapestry needle to score fold lines (see page 15). You can also use it to thread ribbon through holes in some of the projects.

Glue stick This is probably the easiest kind of adhesive to work with.

Hole punch You will use these for punching holes in some of the boxes. The plier kind are probably most useful.

Knitting needle You could use a fairly fine gauge knitting needle instead of a darning needle to score fold lines.

Paper clips Use these to hold two glued surfaces together until the adhesive dries. You can also use small bulldog clips.

Pencil A pencil is best for drawing and marking on paper or card because you can easily rub out what you have drawn if you make a mistake. Use a soft pencil, which is easier to rub out without leaving a mark.

Photocopier If you have access to one, a photocopier is the simplest way to transfer a template to paper or card. It is also an easy way to enlarge or reduce a template, which can then be transferred to paper or card by using carbon paper.

Ruler You will need a ruler for measuring and marking the paper. If you also use it for cutting against, make sure you use a steel rule or one with a metal edge.

Scissors One large pair and one small pair are ideal. Keep them for cutting paper and card.

Set square Use a set square to make sure that the templates you draw are absolutely square.

Spray adhesive Always use this outdoors or in a well-ventilated room. It is extremely useful when you want to stick a sheet of paper to card because it is easy to apply an even coat.

Tracing paper Using tracing paper is the easiest method of transferring a template if you do not have access to a photocopier.

Tweezers A small pair of tweezers can be useful for pressing small folds into place.

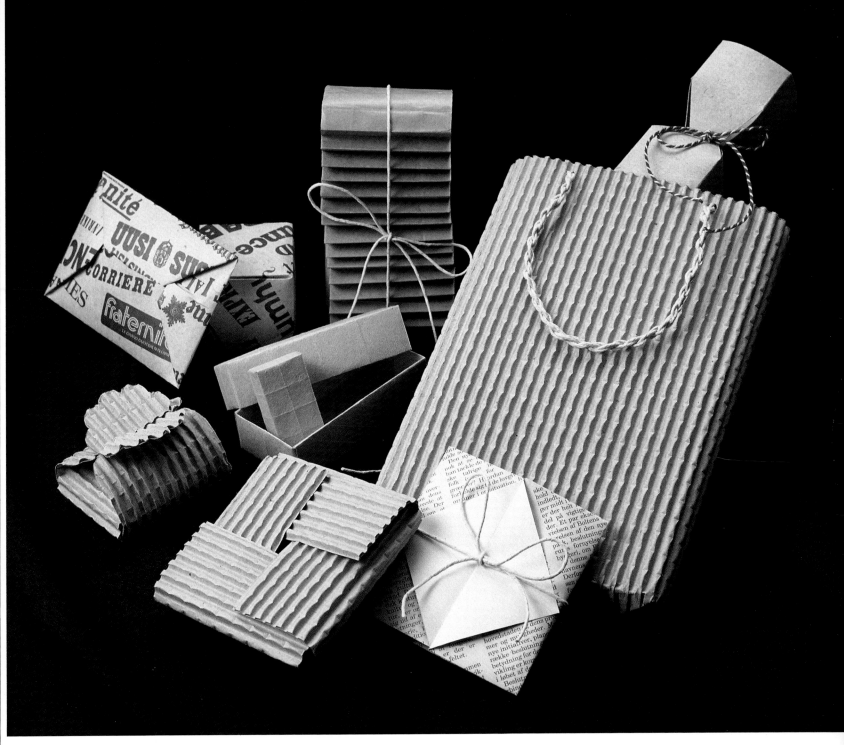

You can use almost any kind of paper or card to make a box.

TEMPLATES

All the patterns for boxes in this book are drawn on a grid so that they can be easily enlarged. If a box consists of, say, six identical sections, in most instances you should draw only one section on the grid, together with any flaps or tabs for gluing and the base. The whole template is always shown small as step 1 in each set of instructions. This also allows you to see how many sections the template consists of.

When you have copied the template section on to tracing paper, you can use carbon paper to transfer it to card, drawing the individual sections side by side to give you the complete template. When there are tabs for gluing or a base section, you need only draw these once. It is vital that you are very careful and precise when you trace over the template. The slightest error at this stage may mean that the box does not turn out properly.

If you want to make several versions of the same box, you will probably find it best to make a template that you can draw around. Use stiff, heavy card. A disadvantage with card is that, as you draw around it, the edges begin to wear and become uneven. If possible, therefore, make the template from stiff plastic, so that the edge remains smooth and even, no matter how many times you cut around it.

The templates can be enlarged by the grid method. All the squares in the book are 1 x 1cm (about $^3/_8$ x $^3/_8$in). To make a template twice as large, draw on a clean sheet of paper a grid with squares 2 x 2cm (about ¾ x ¾in). Choose a starting point on the template drawing and find the equivalent square in your new grid, then simply mark the points where the lines cross the edges of the square. Join the two points with a line as on the template drawing. Continue to copy the template, square by square, until you have transferred the whole outline.

If you have access to a photocopying machine that can enlarge and reduce, you do not need to use the grid method.

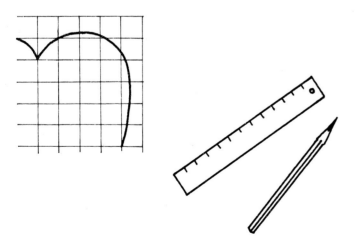

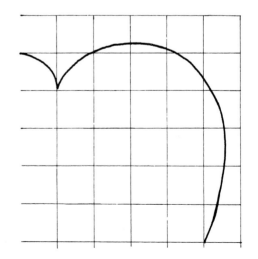

HOW TO FOLD THE BOXES

There is something magical about folding a box and watching it transform itself into the correct shape. When you make the boxes, however, you must always be precise in the cutting and folding, and the various fold lines must always be sharply and neatly defined, otherwise the finished box will be disappointing.

Some of the projects are harder to make than others, although the degree of difficulty is always indicated by the one, two or three small boxes next to the title. You will find that some of the boxes need quite a determined tug to get the folds into the right place, but once you are familiar with a particular box and understand how it works, you will find it much simpler to make.

Some boxes should be folded both up and down – that is, they have "mountain folds" and "valley folds". The term mountain fold means that the wrong sides are facing when the paper

is folded; a valley fold is the opposite - the right sides are facing when the paper is folded. The two kinds of fold are shown on all the templates as follows:

- - - - -   indicates a mountain fold

- · - · -   indicates a valley fold

If you look at the illustrations you will be able to see which way the different lines should be folded.

As we have already noted, it is crucial that the folds are sharply defined. It is a good idea to score the lines by running a darning needle or fine knitting needle against a ruler before folding. Take care that you do not press so hard that the point of your needle goes right through the card.

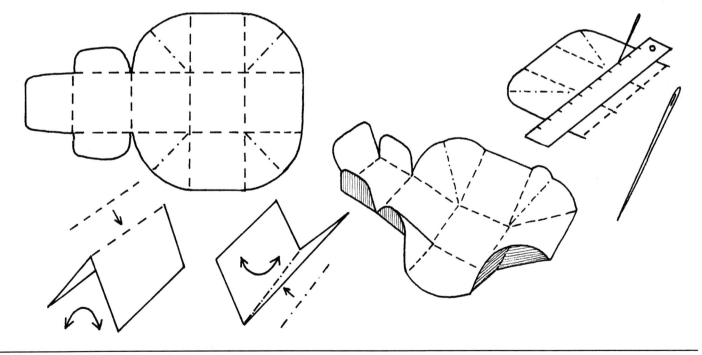

A Simple Parcel [17] 🎁

You can use this method for square or rectangular gifts.

1 Measure right around the object across the shorter sides and take a piece of paper that is about 20cm (8in) longer. The width of the paper should be the same as the object **plus** the depth of the two ends. Fold down the right-hand end of the paper by about 2.5cm (1in).

2 Fold the right-hand end over the object.

3 Fold down the left-hand end of the paper by about 2.5cm (1in) and attach a small piece of double-sided tape to the turned-down edge. Make sure the paper is taut around the object and stick the paper down.

4 Fold down the two ends to make a sharp edge.

5 Fold in the four corners as shown, making sure that the creases are sharp and neat.

6 Attach a piece of double-sided tape to the two free ends before folding the ends up.

7 The wrapped gift.

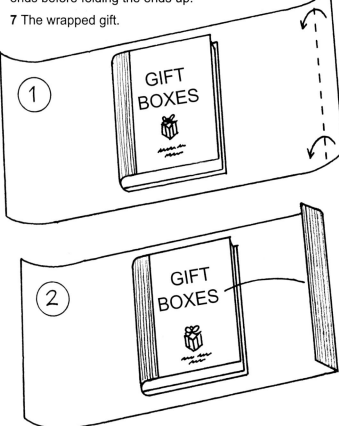

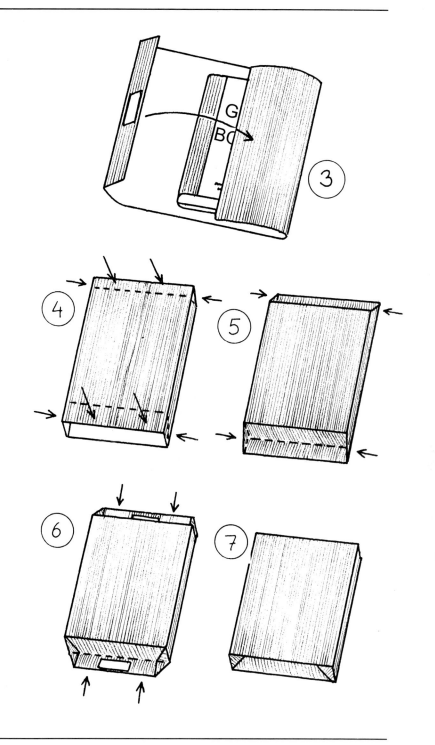

A simple parcel (page 16); concertina-style wrapping (page 18); double-fan wrapping (page 19); wavy-top wrapping (page 19); a parcel with pointed ends (page 26); a bottle in a collar and tie (page 32).

Concertina-style Wrapping [17] 🎁🎁

This type of wrapping is best for a flat, rectangular object such as a book.

1 Measure right around the object along the shorter sides and take a piece of paper that is about 20cm (8in) longer. The paper should be as wide as the object **plus** twice the width. Wrap the paper around the object as described in steps 1–3 on page 16.

2 Press the long ends flat.

3 Neatly fold one end up into concertina folds.

4 Fold the opposite end in the same way, making sure the folds are the same size.

5 Use adhesive tape to hold the opposite corners in position so that the fans open in different directions.

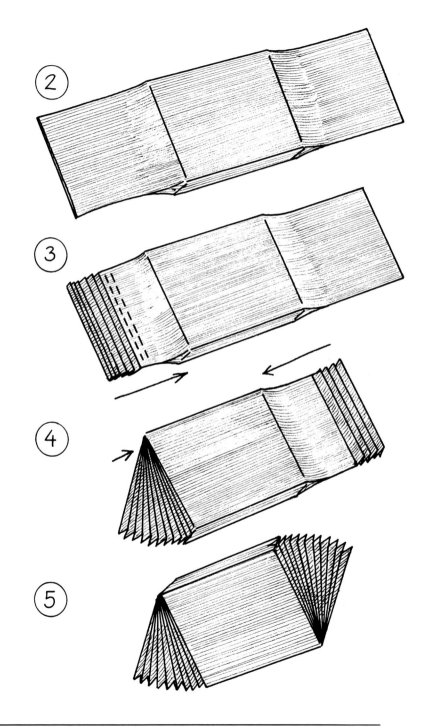

Double-fan Wrapping [17] 🎁 🎁

Use this type of wrapping for flat, rectangular objects.

1 Measure right around the object along the shorter sides and take a piece of paper that is about 20cm (8in) longer. The paper should be as wide as the object **plus** three times the width. Wrap the paper around the object as described in steps 1–3 on page 16. Press the long ends flat, and neatly fold them up into concertina folds. Take a piece of ribbon and run it around the centre of the parcel to press the two ends together.

2 Tie the ribbon in a bow and open out the corners of the fans in towards the middle.

3 Use double-sided tape to hold the fans together in the centre.

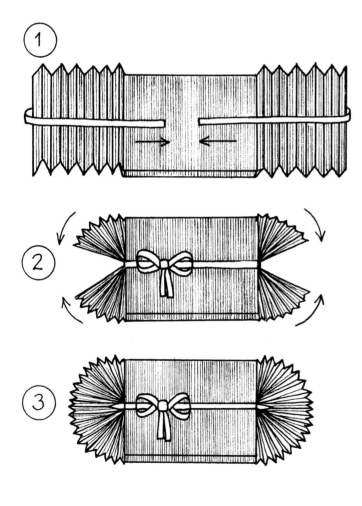

Wavy-top Wrapping [17] [21] 🎁 🎁

This is a suitable method for square or almost square objects.

1 Measure right around the object along the shorter sides and take a piece of paper that is about 20cm (8in) longer. The paper should be about three times the width of the object. Wrap the paper around the object as described in steps 1–3 on page 16, and fold up the bottom end as described in steps 4–6 on page 16.

2 Press the long end flat and fold it up into neat concertina folds, but only as far as the paper will allow. Do not force it.

3 Fold the paper down around the side of the box and hold it in place with a bow.

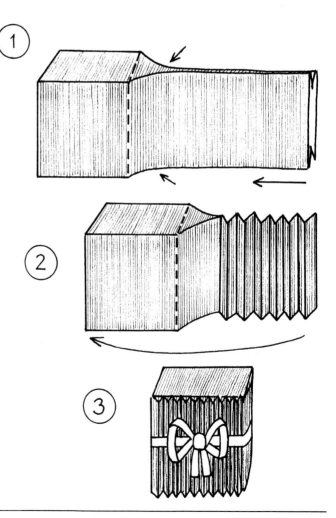

Parcel with a Name Card [21] [25] 🎁🎁

This is suitable for square or rectangular objects.

1 Measure out the paper as described in step 1 on page 16, but allow a little extra paper for the folds around the card. Place the card in the centre of the paper. (Note that only the top section is shown.)

2 Crease the paper up and down to hold and card.

3 Wrap up the parcel as described on page 16.

1 If you prefer you can place the card at an angle. (Note that only the top section is shown.)

2 Fold the paper to hold the card, creasing it neatly.

3 Wrap up the parcel as described on page 16.

① MIKE

② MIKE

③ MIKE

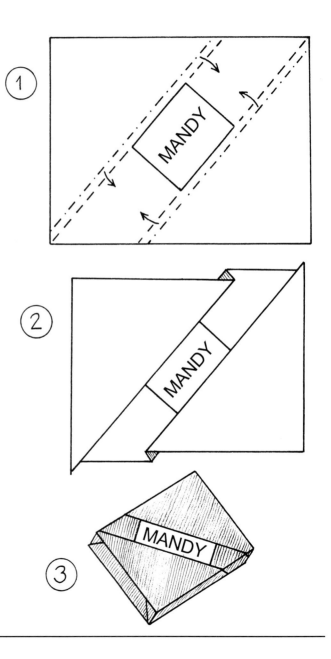

① MANDY

② MANDY

③ MANDY

Wavy-top wrapping (page 19); a parcel with a gift card (page 20); a bottle with wavy wrapping (page 31); a box fastened with ribbon (page 50).

Parcel with a Peacock [25] 🎁🎁🎁

1 Using a piece of paper twice the length of the object, wrap it up as described in steps 1–5 on page 16, but seal the bottom end only.

2 Fold up the free end concertina-style and use a piece of double-sided tape to hold it in place.

3 Open out the fan and use a small piece of double-sided tape to hold the two sides together at the top, leaving a gap for the peacock's body (see step 16).

4 Place a square of paper flat on your work surface and fold two adjacent sides down to the centre fold.

5 Fold the two opposite sides down to the centre.

6 Turn over the paper and fold down the tip to the centre.

7 Fold the top corner down to meet the bottom corner so that the open edges are on top.

8 Fold the left-hand end first to the front, then to the back. Straighten it out.

9 Open the fold and make a mountain fold at each side.

10 Fold back the point. You will have to open out the bottom of the paper slightly.

11–15 Repeat steps 8–10 with the tip of the paper to form the head.

16 Push the body into the centre of the fan and use a piece of double-sided tape to hold it in position.

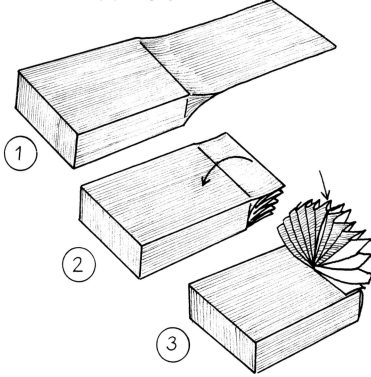

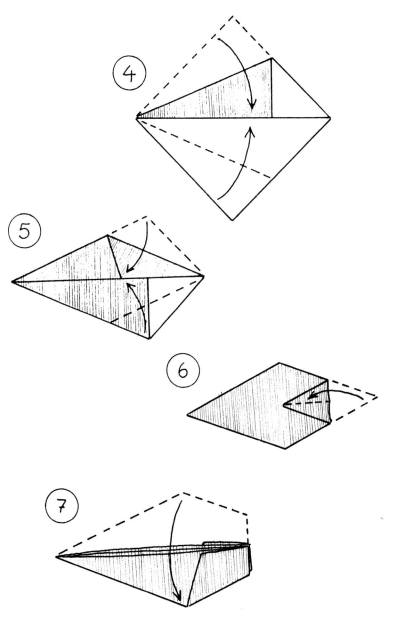

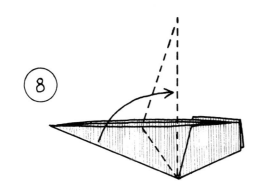

8

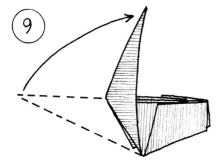

9

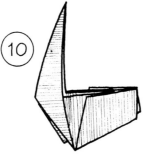

10

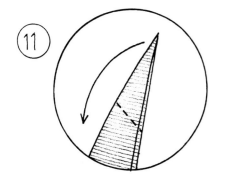

11

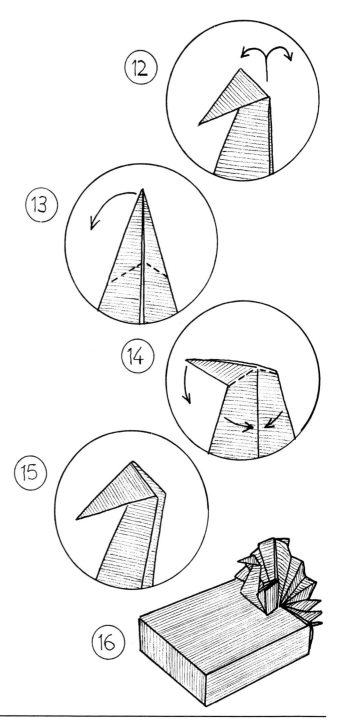

12

13

14

15

16

Parcel with a Triangular Flap [25] 📦 📦

This kind of wrapping works best on flat, rectangular objects.

1 Measure right around the object along the shorter sides and take a piece of paper that is about twice as long as this measurement. The paper should be about one and a half times the width of the object. Lay the object on the paper, about 10cm (4in) from one end.

2 Fold in the two long sides and then fold over the short end. Continue to turn over the object inside the paper until it is completely enclosed.

3 Fold down the top section paper at an angle of 90 degrees.

4 Fold the left-hand flap of paper downwards and in.

B Fold the triangle down over the object.

6 Take the point of the triangle around to the back of the parcel and hold it in place with double-sided tape.

7 Insert a name card into the flap.

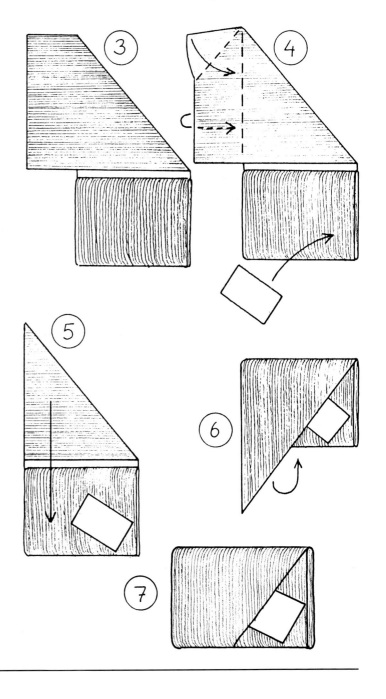

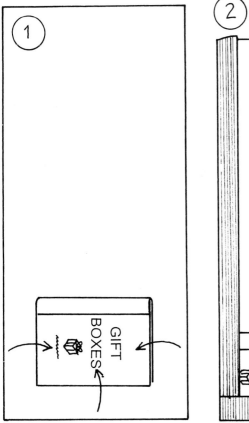

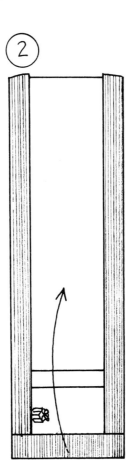

A parcel with a name card (page 20); a parcel with a peacock (page 22); a parcel with a triangular flap (page 24); a parcel with pointed ends (page 26); a gift bag (page 30); a hexagonal parcel for a bottle (page 35).

Parcel with Pointed Ends [17] [25] ☖ ☖

Use this type of wrapping for tall, square or rectangular objects.

1 Measure around the shorter sides of the object and take a piece of paper that is about 20cm (8in) longer than this measurement. The paper should be about three times wider than the object. Wrap up the parcel as described in steps 1–3 on page 16. Press the two long ends flat but make sharp creases along the four folds at each end.

2 Fold over the two ends and hold them down with double-sided tape.

3 Finish off with some ribbon and a simple bow.

1 Measure the paper and wrap up the parcel as in step 1 opposite, but fold in the four edges at each end at an angle as shown.

2 Fold over the ends and hold them down with double-sided tape.

3 Finish off with a length of ribbon and a bow.

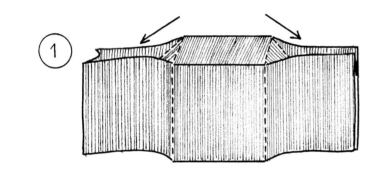

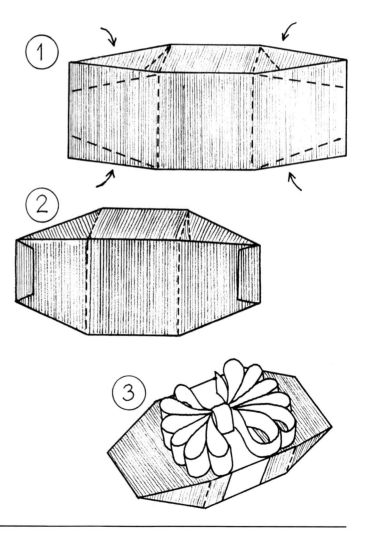

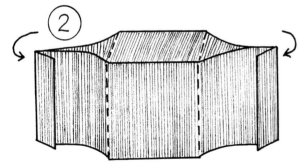

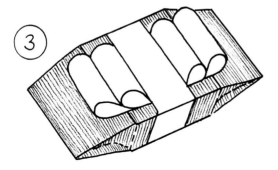

Parcel in a Dinner Jacket [29] ⬦ ⬦

Use paper that is patterned on one side and plain white on the other, or, if you prefer, stick together two differently patterned pieces.

1 The paper should be the same width as the distance around the long sides of the object and about twice as wide as the object.

2 Fold in the two sides so that the join is in the centre and then fold up the bottom end as described in steps 4–6 on page 16. Turn over the parcel.

3 Fold down the top half over the bottom half and hold it in place with double-sided tape.

4 Turn the parcel through 180 degrees.

5 Fold the right-hand middle edge to the right.

6 Repeat on the other side.

7 Fold in the two corners.

8 Crease the small triangles along the line of the lower crease.

9 Fold back the small triangle.

10 Finish off by attaching a bow to the centre top.

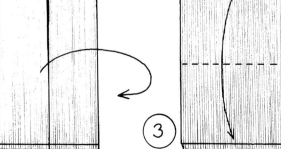

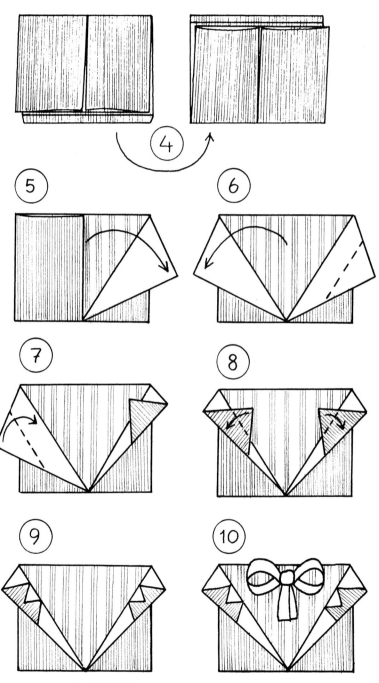

Parcel in a Dress Shirt [29] 🎁🎁

1 Fold the paper in stepped concertina-style as shown in the illustration (only a section of the paper is shown) and use strips of tape to keep the folds in place. When it is folded the paper should be about 20cm (8in) longer than the distance around the object around the shorter sides. The paper needs to be as wide as the object **plus** the depth of the two ends.

2 Wrap up the parcel as described on page 16.

3 Glue three buttons down the front of the parcel.

4 Make the collar from a strip of paper about half as long again as the width of the object. Fold it twice lengthwise.

5 Fold over the ends of the collar and hold them in place with adhesive or double-sided tape.

6 Glue the collar in position.

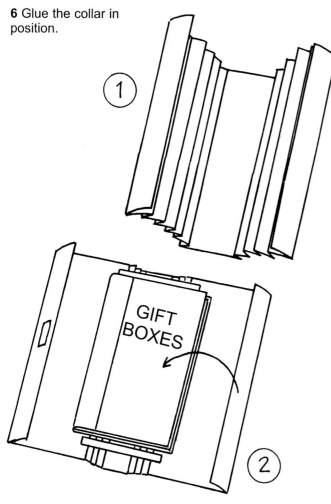

GIFT BOXES

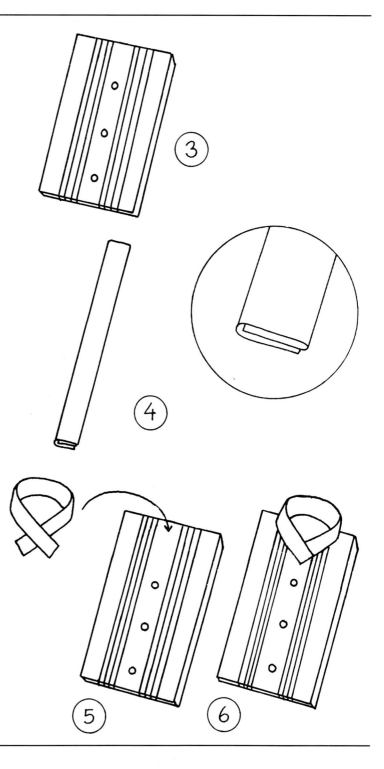

Parcels in a dinner jacket (page 27); parcels in a dress shirt (page 28).

Gift Bag [25] [33] 📦

You can easily make a bag for a small, flat gift by using a thick book to give you the basic shape.

1 Measure around the book across the shorter sides and take a piece of paper about 20cm (8in) longer than this measurement. The paper should be as wide as the book **plus** the depth of the two ends. Fold over the top edge and place the book so that it is flush with the folded edge, then fold over sides, holding the left-hand edge in place with adhesive or double-sided tape.

2 Fold down the bottom end to form a sharp edge.

3 Fold in the two corners as shown

4 Fold up the bottom edge and hold it in place with adhesive or double-sided tape.

5 Take out the book.

6 Punch holes in the top edges.

7 Thread through two loops of cord, knotting them on the inside.

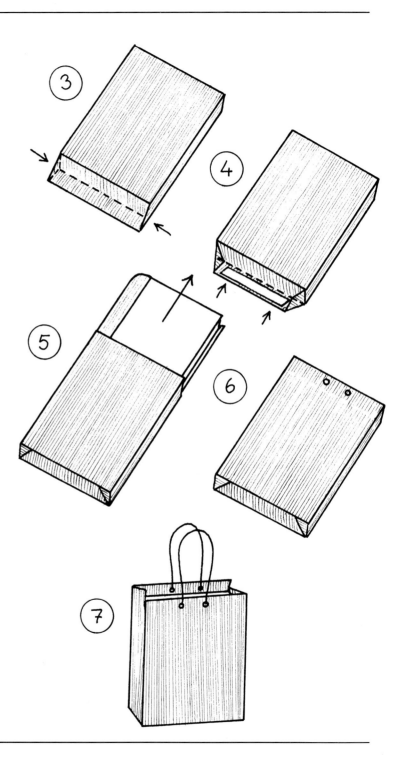

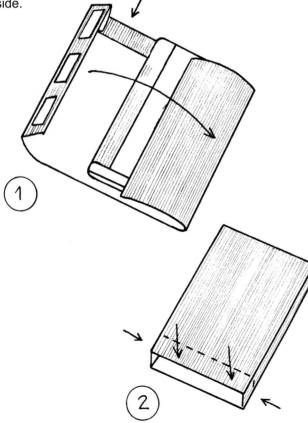

Bottle with Wavy Wrapping [21] [33] 🎁🎁

1 Use a piece of paper that is about three times the height of the bottle and about 10cm (4in) wider than its circumference.

2 Wrap the paper around the bottle and hold the long edges together with double-sided tape or adhesive. Fold under the bottom edge as shown in illustrations A–D.

3 Fold the long end concertina-style.

4 Continue to fold the paper until you reach the top of the bottle.

5 Fold over the top and either hold it down with a piece of double-sided tape or fasten a piece of ribbon tied in a bow around it.

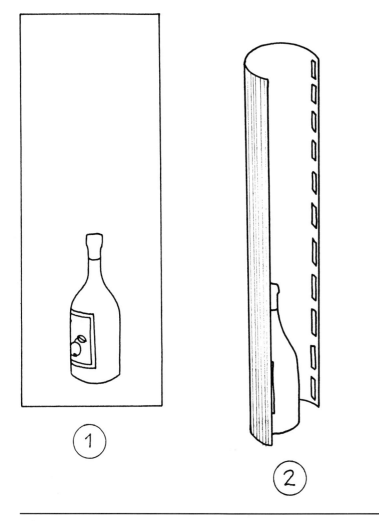

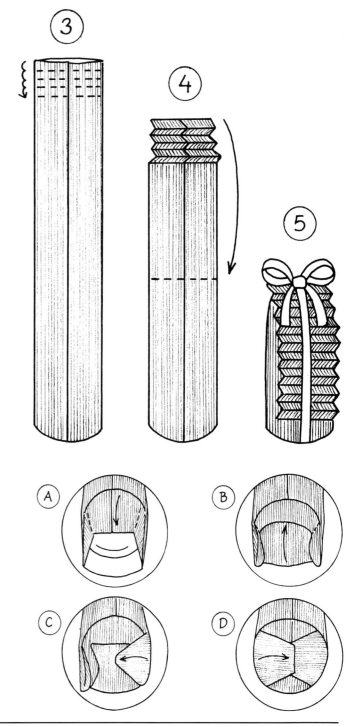

Bottle in a Collar and Tie [17] [33] 🎁🎁

1 Use a piece of paper that is about twice the height of the bottle and about 10cm (4in) wider than its circumference.

2 Wrap the paper around the bottle and fold under the bottom edge as described in step 2 on page 31.

3 Use a piece of silk ribbon 30–35cm (12–14in) long for the tie and fold the top edge of the paper down over the ribbon, holding it in place with adhesive or double-sided tape.

4 Carefully cut the paper below the fold on both sides.

5 Fold the collar forwards and the two corners backwards, smoothing the collar into shape. If you wish, knot the tie as shown below (illustrations A–D), cut off any excess ribbon and trim the bottom edges to points.

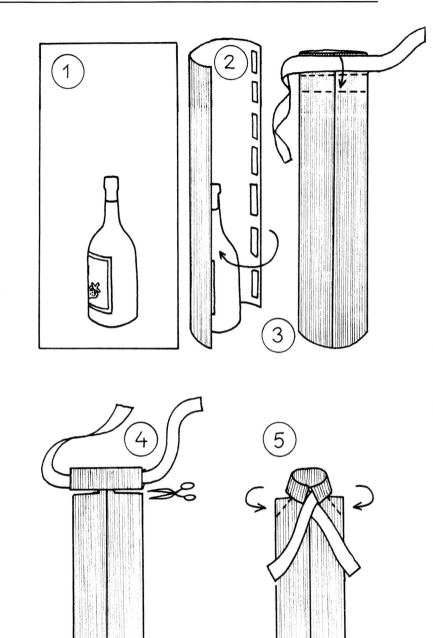

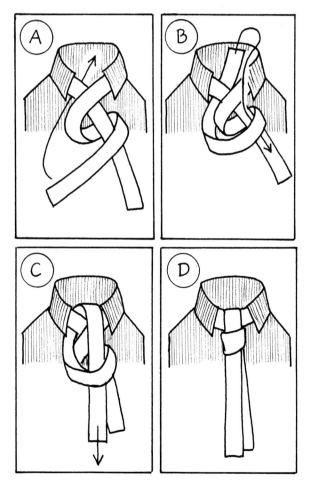

A gift bag (page 30); a bottle with wavy wrapping (page 31); a bottle in a collar and tie (page 32); a bottle with a spiral top (page 34); a bottle with a fan (page 34); a box with a curved top (page 46); a folder with flaps (page 52); a tobacco pouch (page 71).

Bottle with a Spiral Top [33] 🎁🎁

1 Use a piece of paper that is about twice the height of the bottle and 10cm (4in) wider than its circumference.

2 Wrap the paper around the bottle and fold under the bottom edge as described in step 2 on page 31.

3 Press the top section flat, folding in the side sections.

4 Start at the top and make a tight roll.

5 Pull one of the inside corners out to one side.

Bottle with a Fan [33] 🎁🎁

1 Use a piece of paper that is about half as long again as the height of the bottle and about 10cm (4in) wider than its circumference.

2 Roll the paper around the bottle as shown so that the large triangle points upwards.

3 Turn the bottle so that the triangle points to the left.

4 Fold up the triangle concertina-style.

5 Press the folds together and hold them in place with adhesive or double-sided tape.

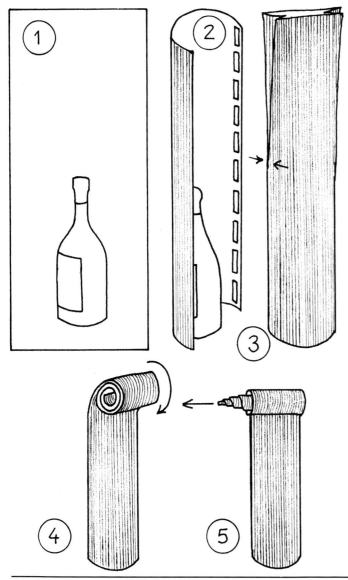

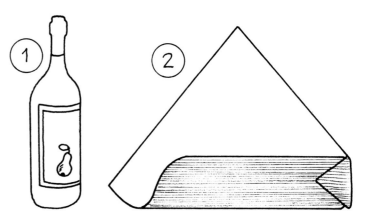

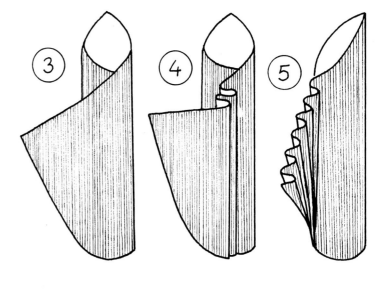

Hexagonal Parcel for a Bottle [25] 🎁🎁

Although the instructions will make a container for a standard-shaped bottle, you could use it for other things.

1 Copy the template and transfer it to a piece of card six times, drawing the bottom section as shown.

2 Check that your bottle will fit, then score the fold lines. Turn up the flaps around the base.

3 Use adhesive or double-sided tape to hold the tabs together and place the bottle inside.

4 Use a piece of ribbon to tie around the neck.

5 Tie a neat bow, trimming the ends even.

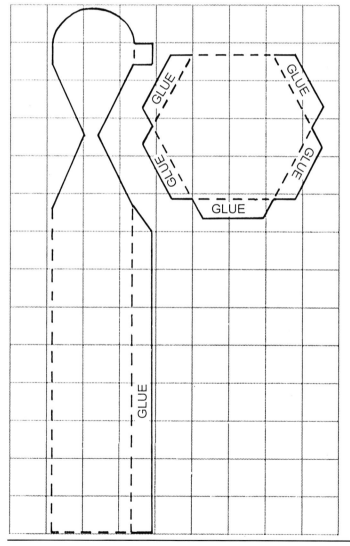

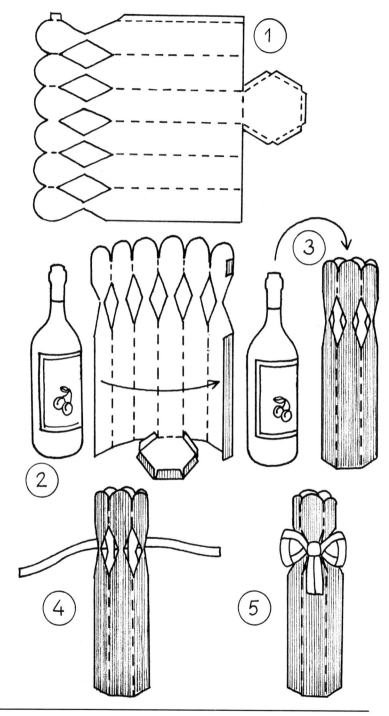

Double Bow [37] 📦📦

Use two equal lengths of ribbon. The lengths will determine the final size, so practise with shorter pieces. Use synthetic ribbon, which holds its shape better than silk.

1 Form the ribbon into a loop and hold the end with a small piece of double-sided tape.

2 Make a slightly larger loop and, again, hold it in place with a small piece of double-sided tape.

3 When you have made the third loop, cut the ribbon. If you want a larger bow, keep on adding loops, folding and sticking them as before.

4 Make a second bow, the same size as the first, and place them at right-angles, holding them together with adhesive or double-sided tape.

5 Attach the bow to the top of the wrapped gift.

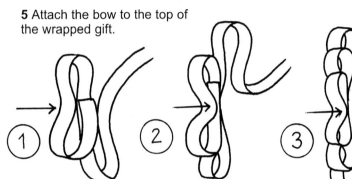

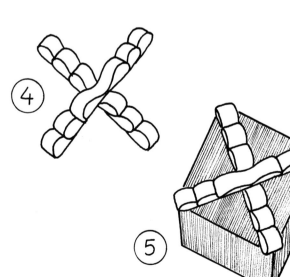

Rosette [37] 📦📦

You will need a fairly long piece of ribbon. Use synthetic ribbon rather than silk because it keeps its shape better.

1 Form the ribbon into a single loop and hold it in place with a small piece of double-sided tape.

2 Make another loop to form a figure-of-eight.

3 Repeat the previous steps until you have made twelve, evenly sized loops.

4 Hold the loops together with a little piece of ribbon, glued into place.

5 Attach the rosette to the top of the wrapped gift.

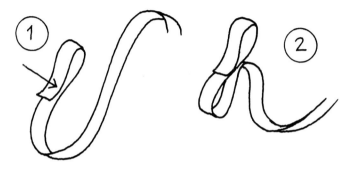

A double bow (page 36); a rosette (page 36); a flower bow (page 38); a multiple bow (page 38); a shell-shaped bow (page 39); a loose bow (page 39).

Flower Bow [37] 🎁 🎁

You should use narrow synthetic ribbon, which is stiff enough to stand upright.

1 Wind the ribbon fifteen to twenty times around a piece of card, then cut through both ends so that you have lots of small pieces, all the same length.

2 Tie these pieces tightly together around the centre.

3 Make a second bunch in exactly the same way and place the two bunches at right-angles to each other. Tie them firmly together.

4 Arrange the lengths of ribbon to look like petals and then glue the bow to the top of the wrapped gift.

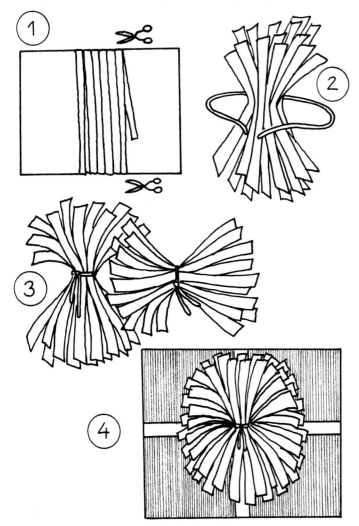

Multiple Bow [37] 🎁 🎁

You will need eight pieces of synthetic ribbon, four pieces about 20cm (8in) long, three pieces about 15cm (6in) long and one piece about 5cm (2in) long.

1 Use adhesive or double-sided tape to hold the long pieces of ribbon together.

2 Place the folded ribbons in a star shape, holding them together with spots of adhesive or little pieces of double-sided tape. Do the same with the three medium pieces, then fasten them to the centre of the larger star.

3 Make a loop out of the short piece of ribbon and stick it to the centre of the star.

4 Glue the whole bow to the wrapped gift.

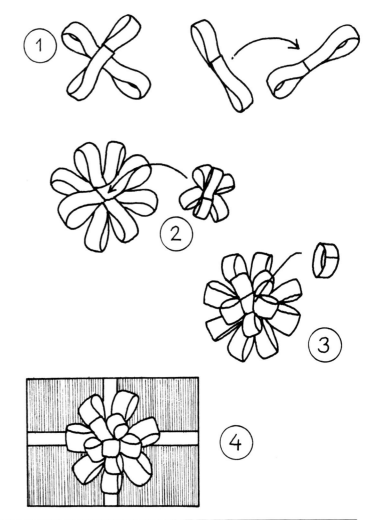

Shell-shaped Bow [37] 🎁 🎁

You will need six pieces of synthetic ribbon for this bow, they should be about 10cm (4in), 12cm (4½in), 14cm (5½in), 16cm (6½in), 18cm (7¼in) and 20cm (8in) long.

1 Fold the longest piece of ribbon into a twisted figure-of-eight as shown and fasten it with a small piece of double-sided tape.

2 Repeat step 1 with the other pieces of ribbon, then use double-sided tape to hold the figures-of-eight together.

3 Attach the bow to the top of the wrapped gift.

Loose Bow [37] 🎁 🎁

Use two lengths of synthetic ribbon, one of which should be about two-thirds of the length of the other.

1 Fold the longer length of ribbon as shown and use double-sided tape to hold it in place.

2 Fold the shorter length of ribbon as shown and use double-sided tape to hold it in place.

3 Place the two pieces together.

4 Hold them together with double-sided tape.

5 Attach the finished bow to the top of the wrapped gift.

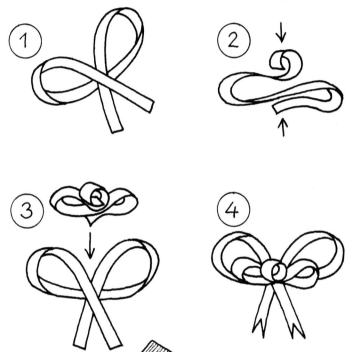

Triangular Heart [41]

1 Copy and cut out the template and score along the fold lines.

2 Bend the card along the score lines and glue the tab and side together.

3 The finished heart.

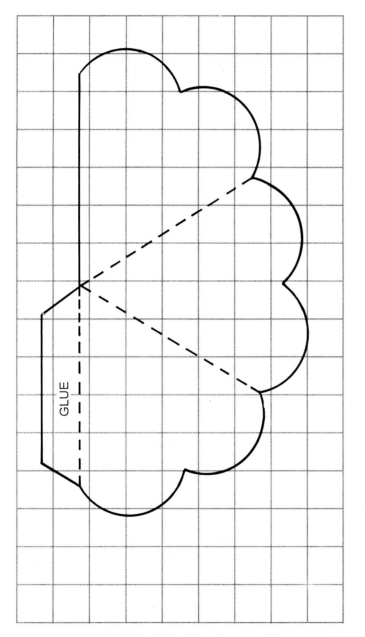

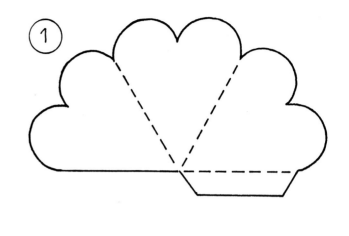

GLUE

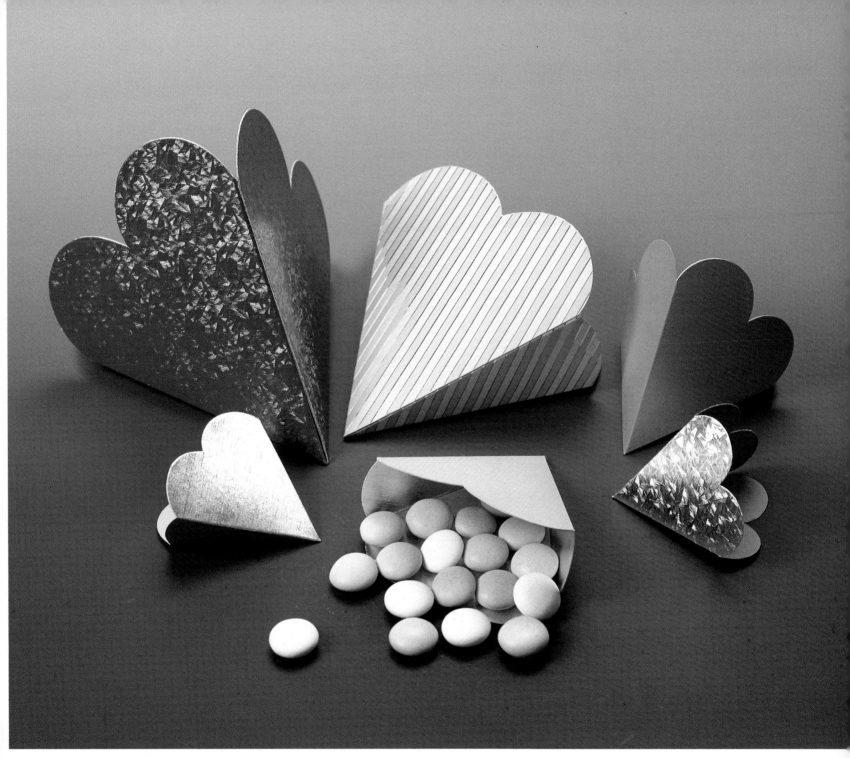

Triangular hearts (page 40); four-sided hearts (page 42).

Four-sided Heart [41] ⬦

1 Copy and cut out the template and score along the fold lines.

2 Bend the card along the score lines and glue the tab and side together.

3 The finished heart.

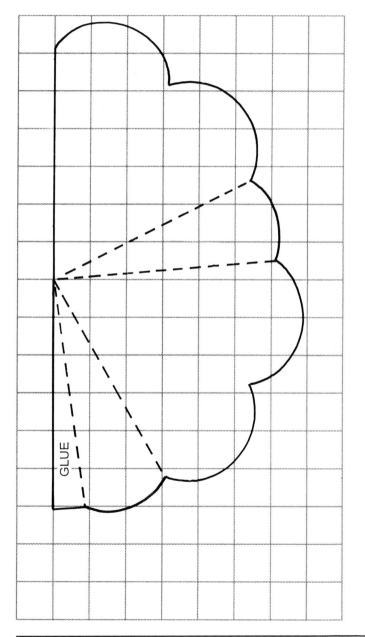

GLUE

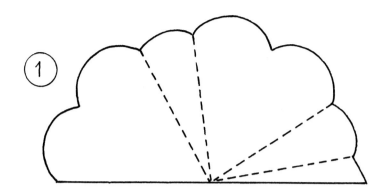

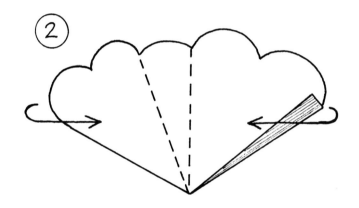

Box with Curved Flaps [45]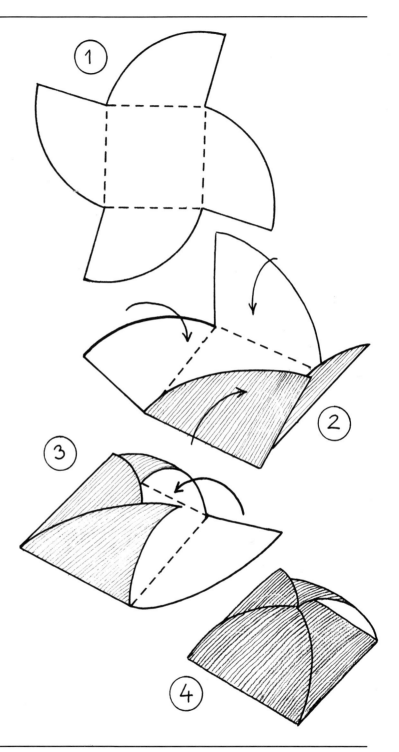

1 Copy the template and transfer it twice to a piece of card, matching up the centre line exactly. Cut out the shape and score along the fold lines.

2 Fold the four flaps in towards the centre.

3 Fold the flaps in over each other, as you would do if you were closing an ordinary cardboard box.

4 The finished box.

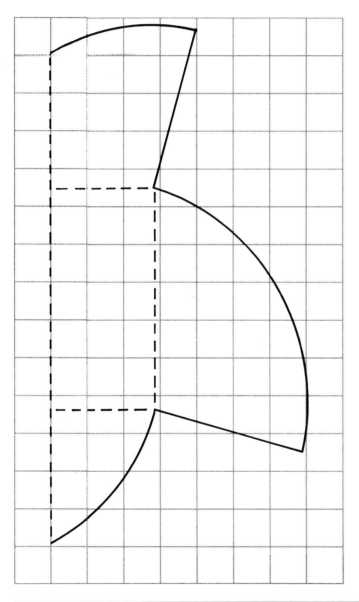

Box with Rosette Flaps [45]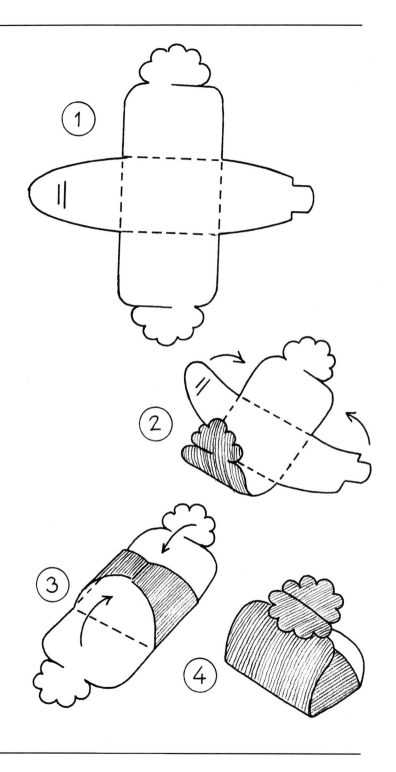

1 Copy the template and transfer it twice to a piece of card, matching up the centre line exactly. Cut out the shape and score along the fold lines.

2 Fold the two sides pieces towards the centre.

3 Insert the flap through the slit in the opposite side, then fold the two rosettes towards the centre.

4 Slot the notches into each other to hold the rosettes together.

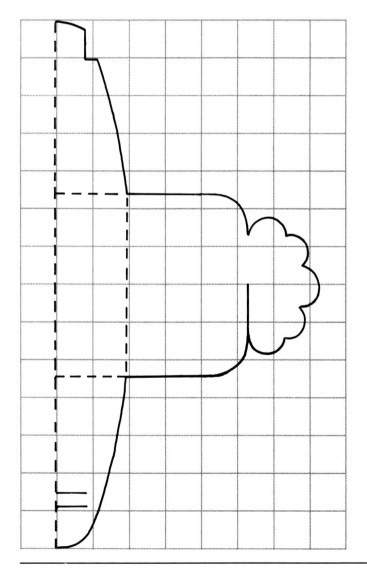

Boxes with curved flaps (page 43); boxes with rosette flaps (page 44); boxes with curved tops (page 46).

45

Box with a Curved Top [33] [45] [61]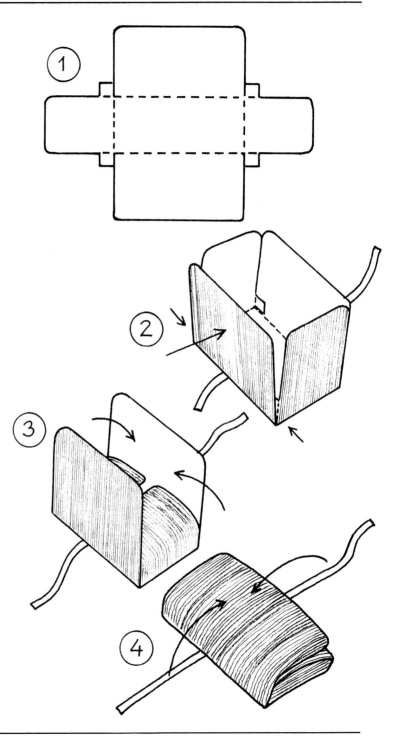

1 Copy the template and transfer it twice to a piece of card, matching up the centre line exactly. Cut out the shape and score along the fold lines.

2 Fold the sides upwards and towards the centre and glue the flaps.

3 Fold over the two side pieces, forming them into gentle curves. Take care that the card does not crack.

4 Fold over the other two sides and hold them in place with a ribbon. When the box has been standing for a while, you can press the sides into shape.

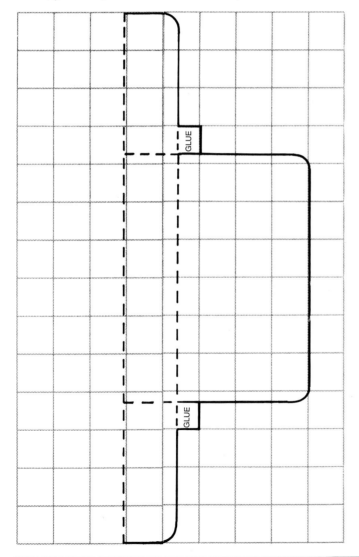

GLUE

GLUE

Oval Box [49]

1 Copy the template and transfer it twice to a piece of card, matching up the centre line exactly. Cut out the shape and score along the fold lines.

2 Glue the long edges together with the flap inside.

3 Bend the top ends and fold them inwards.

4 Repeat step 3 at the other end.

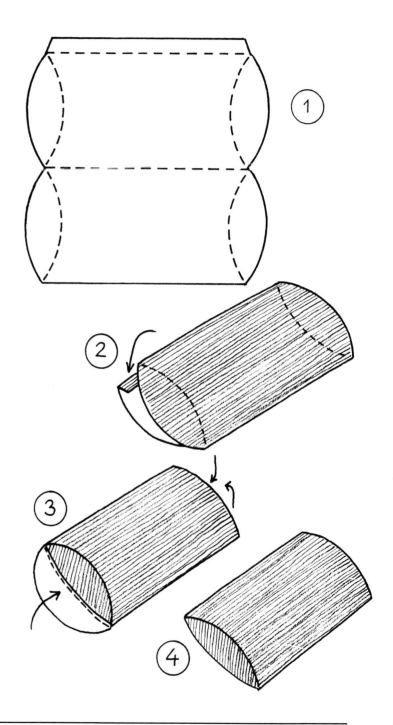

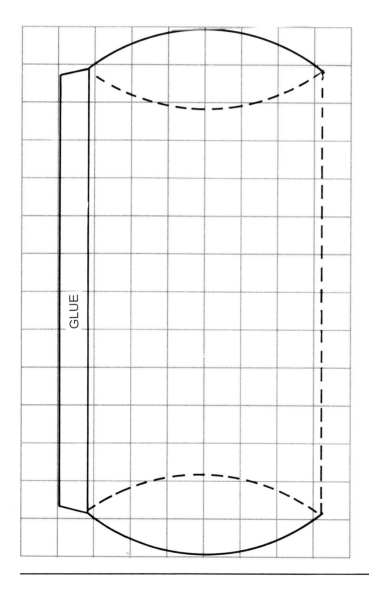

GLUE

Simple Pyramid Box [49]

1 Copy the template and transfer it twice to a piece of card, matching up the centre line exactly. Cut out the shape and score along the fold lines.

2 Fold up two opposite sides and fold in the narrow flaps.

3 Fold up the other sides in the same way.

4 Thread a piece of fine cord through the holes to close the box.

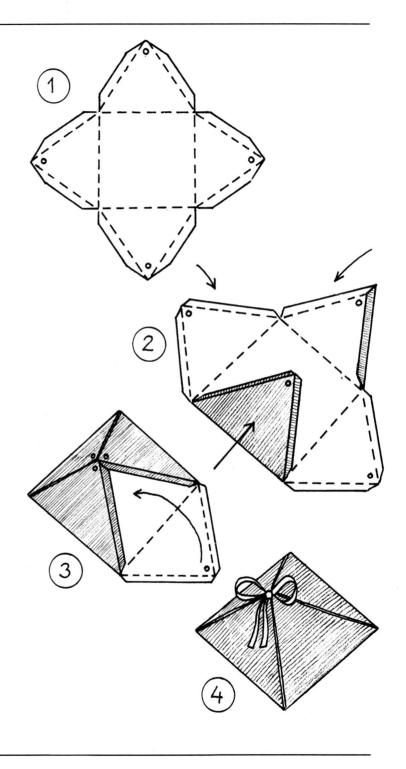

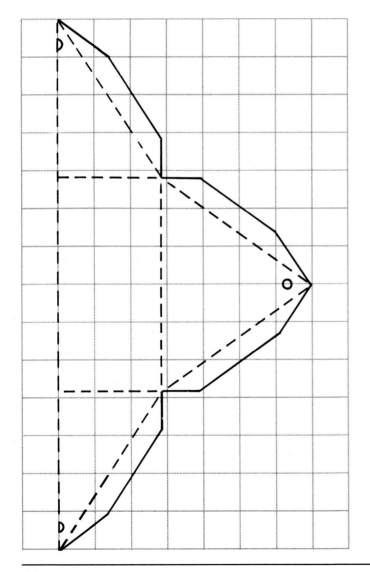

Oval boxes (page 47); simple pyramid boxes (page 48); boxes trimmed with ribbon (page 51).

Box Fastened with Ribbon [21]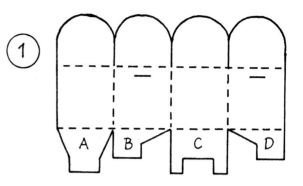

1 Transfer the template to card and cut out the shape. Score along the fold lines.

2 Fold along the lines and glue the flap to the other end.

3 The flaps at the bottom are identified by letters in figure 1. Fold C inwards; fold B and D over C; push A into the slot.

4 Thread ribbon through the slots, fold down the side flaps, then the two top flaps. Hold the flaps down by tying a neat bow.

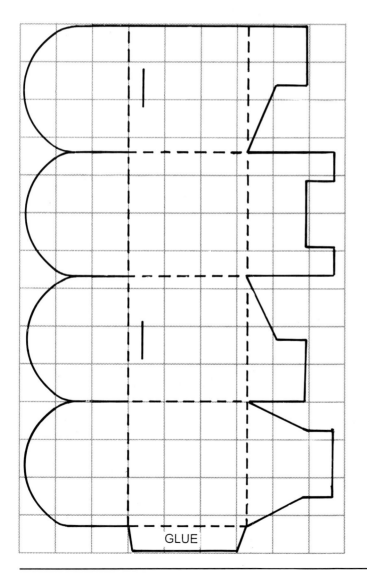

GLUE

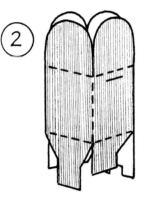

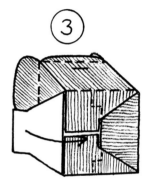

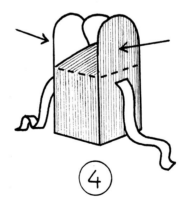

Box Trimmed with Ribbon [49]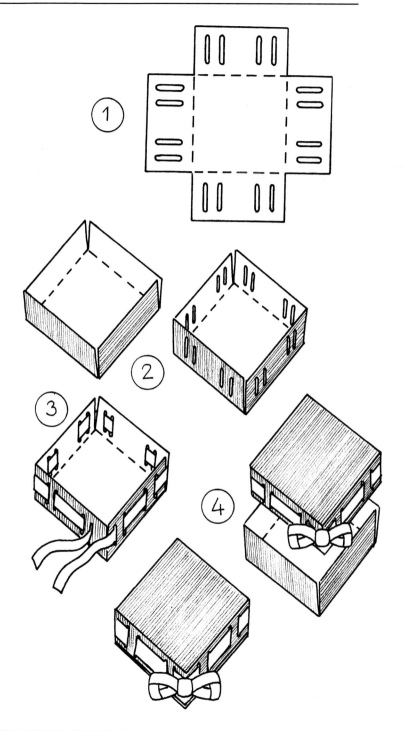

1 Copy the template and transfer it twice to a piece of card, matching up the centre line exactly. Cut out two shapes and score along the fold lines. Cut out slots for the ribbon in one of the pieces only.

2 Fold up the sides of the two pieces, one of which will be the base.

3 Thread ribbon through the slots in the top piece. Ideally, the ribbon should be the same width as the slots.

4 Tie the ribbon in a bow to hold the base and top together.

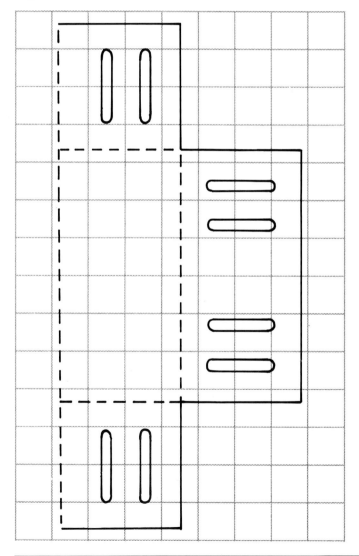

Folder with Flaps [33] [53] 📦

To make this folder you need two pieces of paper or card, each twice as long as they are wide.

1 Carefully measure and mark three equidistant points along each edge and mark two fold lines on the outer marks. Score along the fold lines.

2 Lay one piece of card over the other so that they are at right-angles.

3 Bend up one of the flaps of the bottom piece of card.

4 Bend up the second flap.

5 Bend up the next flap and then, as you would when closing a cardboard box, fold the final flap so that half of it lies under the first flap.

6 The finished folder.

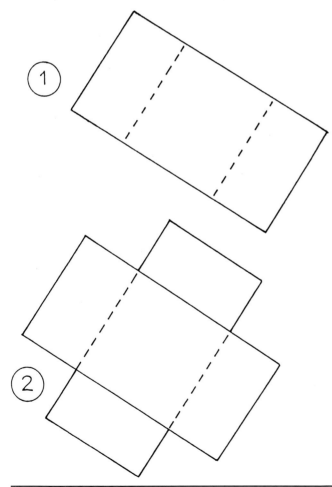

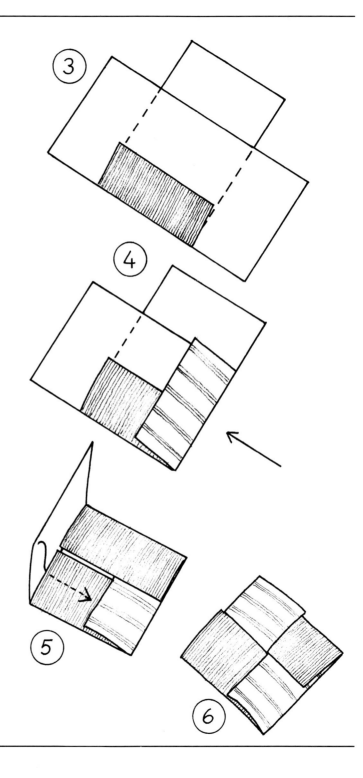

Folders with flaps (page 52); a pyramid box (page 60); closing boxes (pages 66).

53

Folder with Slotted Flap [57] ⬡

1 Transfer the template to card. Cut out the shape and score along the fold lines. Fold in the two short edges.

2 Fold over the left-hand edge.

3 Fold the right-hand edge over to the centre.

4 Insert the flap in the slot.

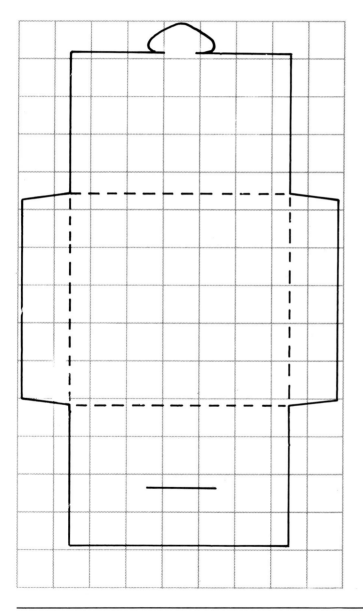

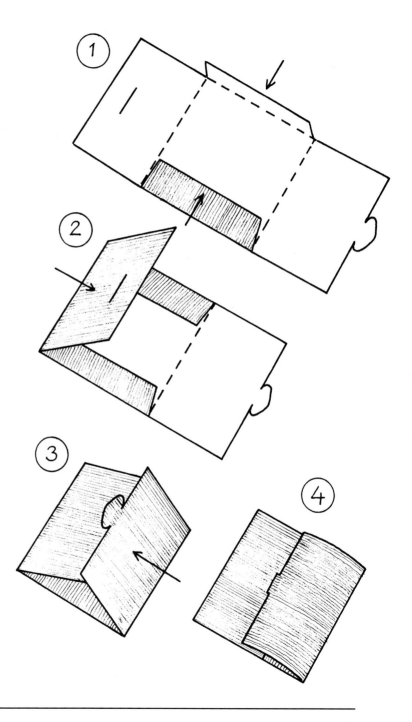

Envelope [57]

1 Take a square piece of paper and fold it as shown.

2 Fold the bottom edge up to the centre.

3 Fold in the outside edges to the centre.

4 Fold under the two bottom corners.

5 Fold the two top corners down towards the centre as shown.

6 Fold down the top triangle.

7 Tuck the point of the triangle under the flap.

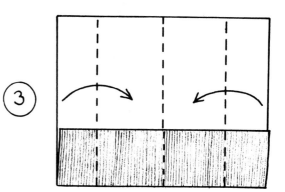

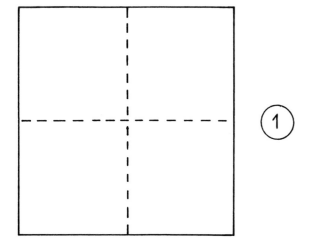

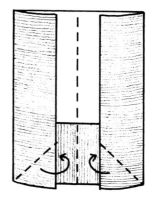

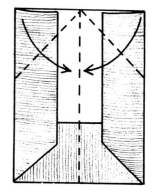

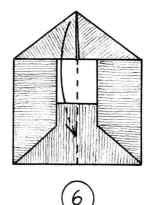

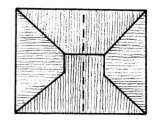

Japanese-style Folder [57]

This will look especially effective if you use paper that has a different colour or pattern on each side.

1 Take a square of paper and fold it in half as shown.

2 Fold the resulting triangle as shown.

3 Open out the paper and fold it again as shown.

4 Fold the left-hand corner towards the right.

5 Fold the right-hand corner towards the left.

6 Fold down the top corner.

7 Fold up the point of the top flap.

8 Fold up the bottom flap and then fold down the point.

9 Tie a piece of ribbon around the folder.

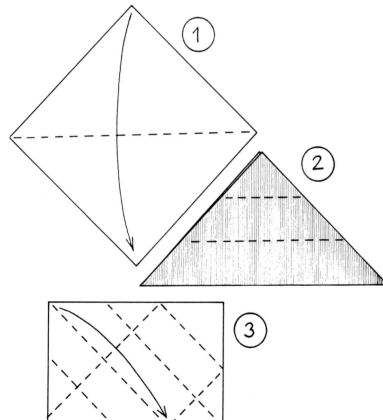

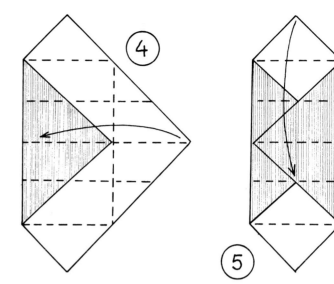

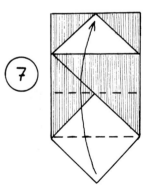

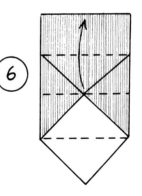

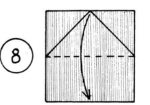

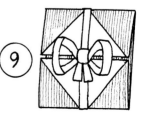

Folder with slotted flap (page 54); envelope (page 55); Japanese-style folders (page 56); twin-peaked triangular boxes (page 76).

Rectangular Box Made from a Circle [61] 📦📦

If you use two circles you can make a base and a lid.

1 Fold the circle as shown.

2 Fold up the bottom part of the circle.

3 Fold the lower section up towards the centre and fold down the top towards the centre.

4 Fold down the top section to the centre.

5 Open out the circle and turn it through 90 degrees.

6 Fold up the bottom section towards the centre.

7 Repeat steps 3-5.

8 Open out the circle and cut it as shown.

9 Turn in the top and bottom folds towards the centre.

10 Lift the sides and bend the corners inwards to form the shape of the box.

11 Fold in the right- and left-hand sections, holding them in place with glue or double-sided tape if you wish.

12 The base of the box is ready. Start again from the beginning to make the top.

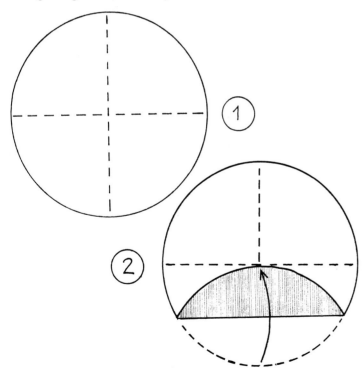

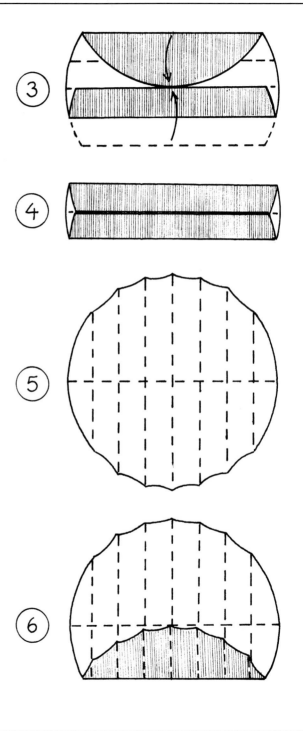

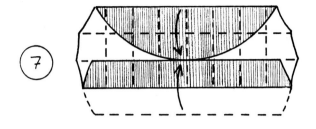

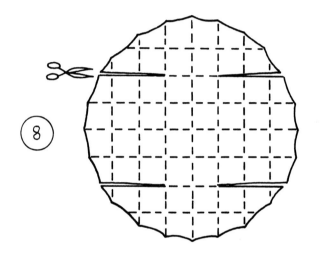

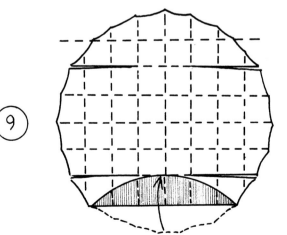

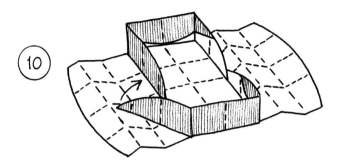

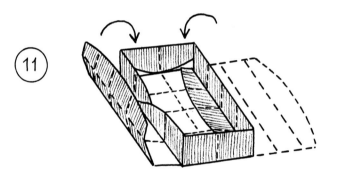

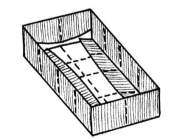

Pyramid Box [53] [61]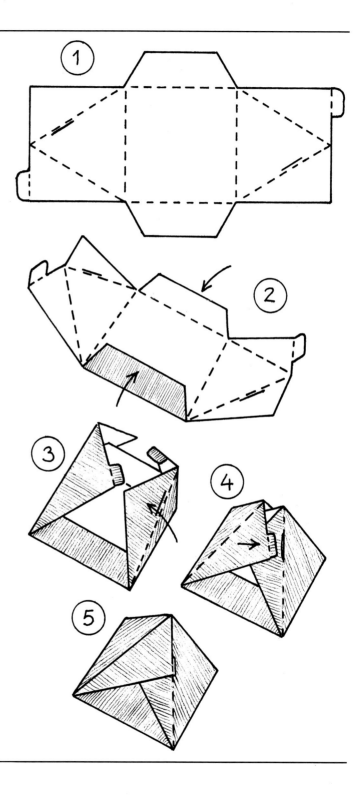

1 Copy the template and transfer it twice to a piece of card, matching up the centre line exactly. Cut out the shape and score along the fold lines.

2 Fold in the two short sides towards the centre.

3 Fold in the triangular sides towards the centre.

4 Push the tabs into the corresponding slots.

5 The finished pyramid.

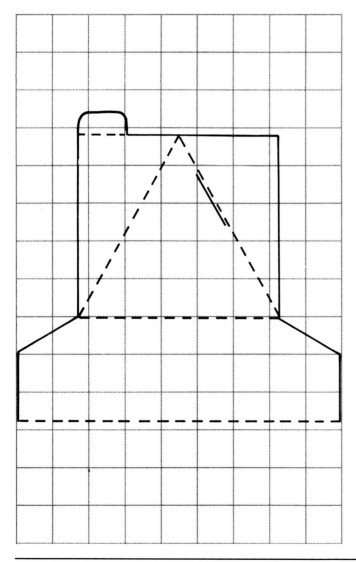

A box with a curved top (page 46); rectangular boxes made from circles (page 58); pyramid boxes (page 60).

Box with Handle [65] 📦 📦

1 Copy the template and transfer it twice to a piece of card, matching up the centre line exactly. Cut out the shape and score along the fold lines.

2 Fold in the two short sides towards the centre so that the handle flaps point upwards.

3 Fold down the other sides so that the slots fit over the handles.

4 The finished box.

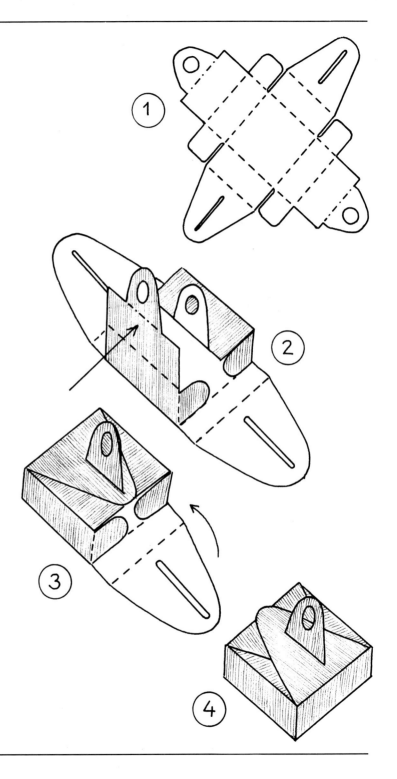

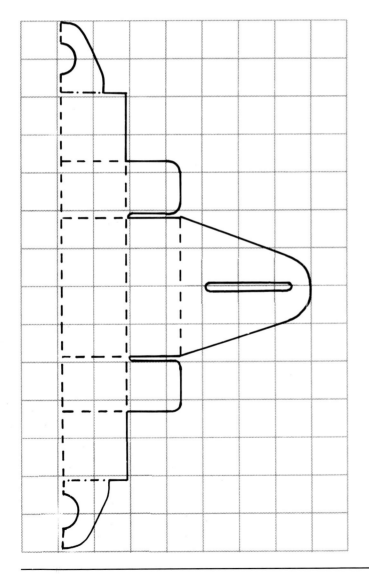

62

Small Box with Curved Flaps [65]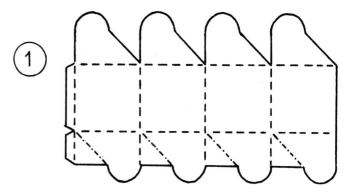

1 Copy the template and transfer it four times to the card, placing each shape next to the other. Cut out the shape and score along the fold lines.

2 Glue the sides together.

3 Fold over the four flaps at the bottom, slotting them together to make the base.

4 Turn the box the right way up and fold down the top flaps.

5 The finished box.

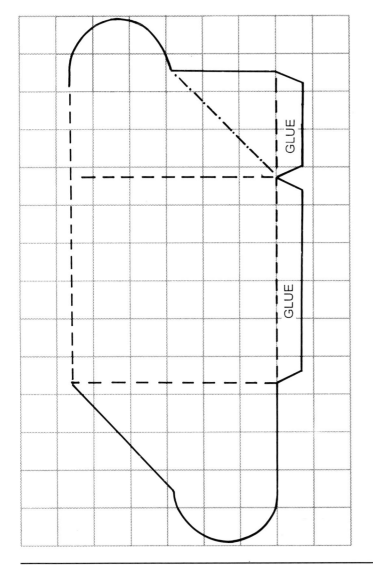

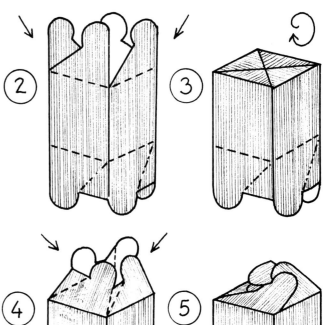

Oblong Folding Box [65] 📦 📦

1 Copy the template and transfer it four times to the card, placing each shape next to the other. Cut out the shape and score along the fold lines.

2 Fold the box by pressing one side at a time into shape.

3 Begin to fold the box into shape.

4 Push the final section into the bottom corner.

5 The finished box.

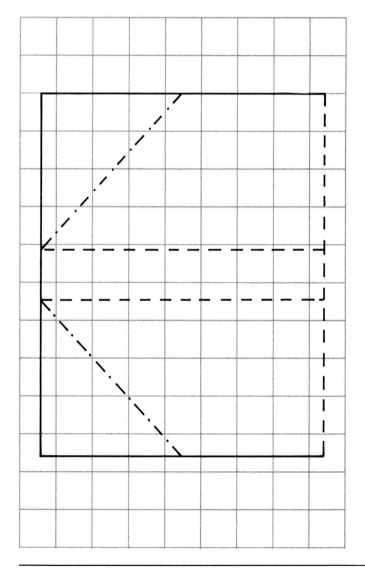

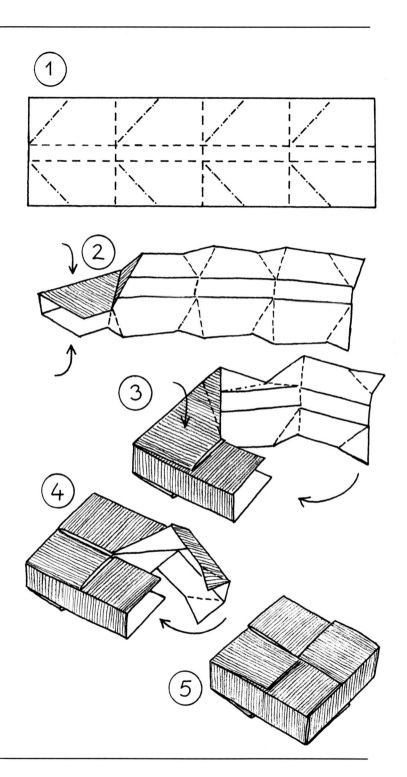

Boxes with handles (page 62); small boxes with curved flaps (page 63); oblong folding boxes (page 64); hexagonal boxes with spiral flaps (page 74).

65

Closing Box [53] 📦 📦

You could make the box out of black or white card and decorate it with spots to resemble a die.

1 Transfer the template to card. Cut out the shape and score along the fold lines.

2 Fold the four rounded corners inwards.

3 Press in the valley folds neatly and carefully.

4 Push the sides upwards.

5 Fold the lid down and slot in the tab to close the box.

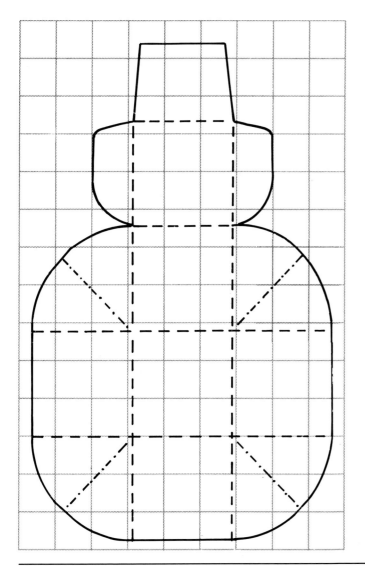

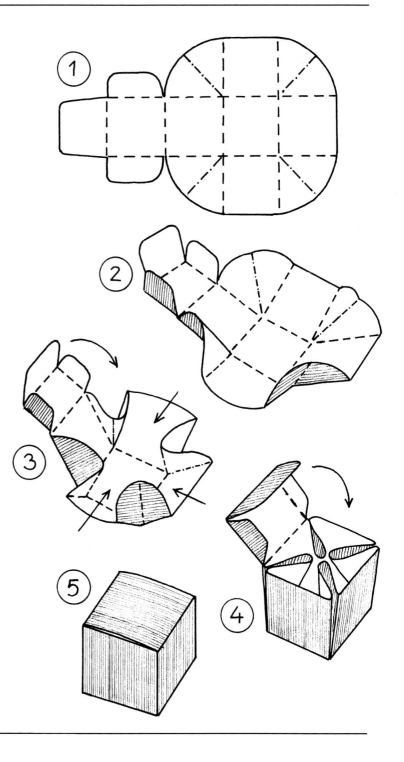

Cone-shaped Box with Rosette [69] ⬡ ⬡ ⬡

1 Transfer the template to card, placing six outlines next to each other. Cut out the shape and score along the fold lines.

2 Fold the box and glue the sides together.

3 Fold the flaps inwards, over each other.

4 The last flap holds everything together.

5 When the flaps are folded together, the top looks like a rosette.

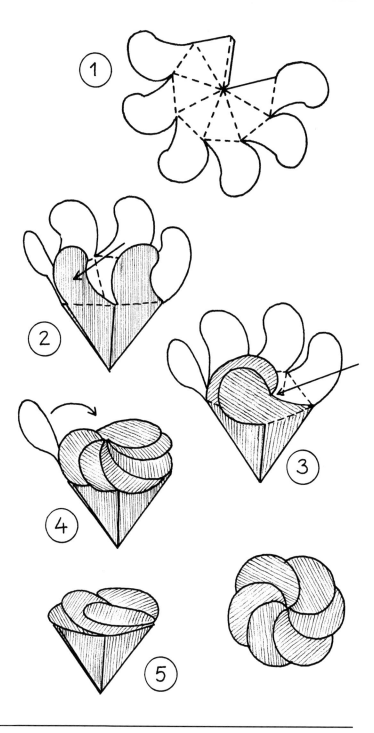

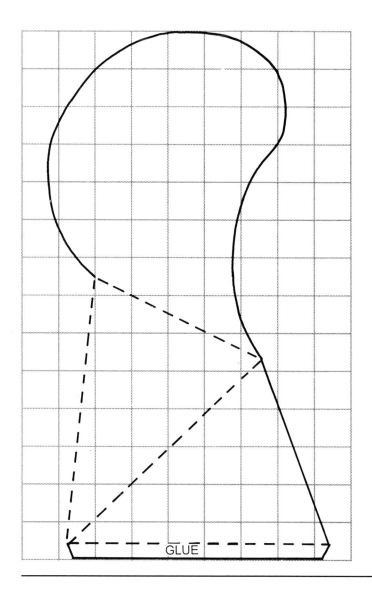

GLUE

Pentagonal Box with Flower [69] 🗔 🗔 🗔

1 Transfer the template to card, placing five outlines around the pentagon. Cut out the shape and score along the fold lines.

2 Fold in the five flaps.

3 Fold the flaps over each other as shown.

4 The last flap holds the box together.

5 The finished box.

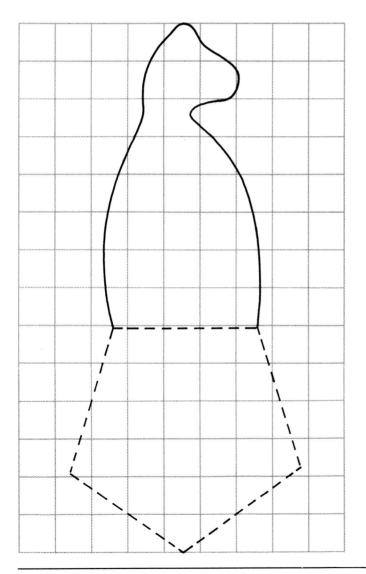

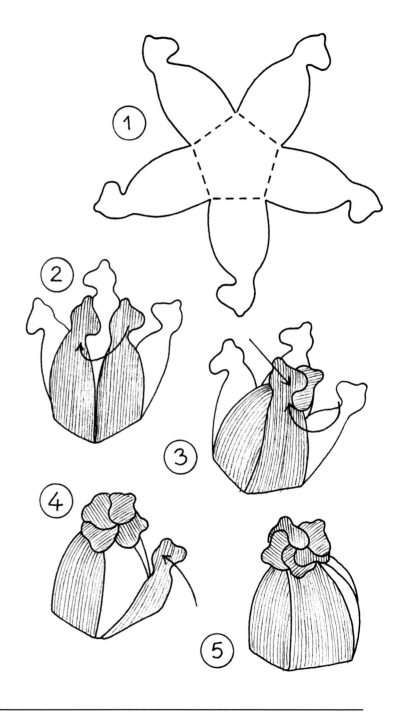

Cone-shaped boxes with rosettes (page 67); pentagonal boxes with flowers (page 68); hexagonal boxes (page 70).

Hexagonal Box [69]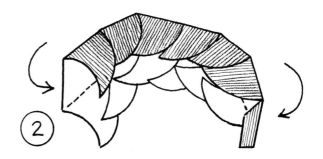

1 Transfer the template to card, placing six outlines next to each other as shown. Cut out the shape and score along the fold lines.

2 Fold the box, bending it carefully into shape.

3 Glue the box together.

4 The top and bottom of the box should be identical.

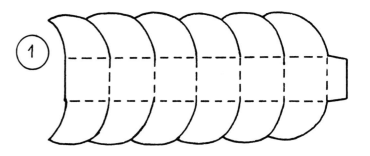

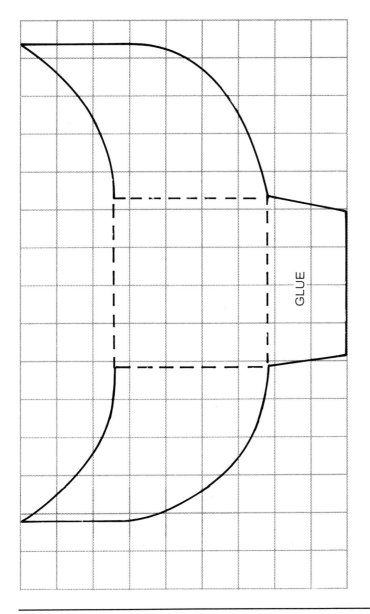

GLUE

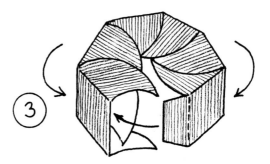

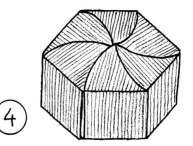

Tobacco Pouch [33] [73]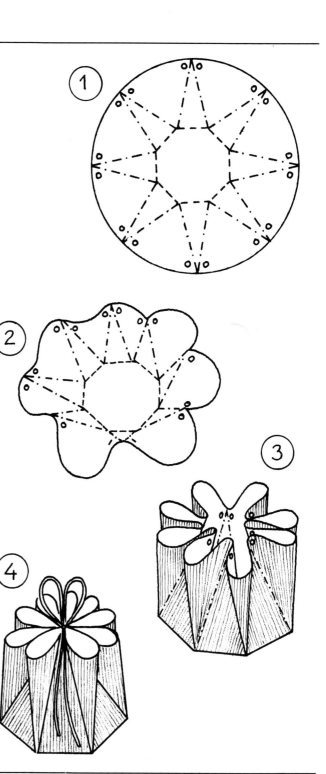

1 Copy the template and transfer it twice to a piece of card, matching up the centre line exactly. Cut out the shape and score along the fold lines. Punch out the holes.

2 Press up and inwards along the fold lines.

3 The corners should come together in the centre.

4 Thread a piece of cord through the holes.

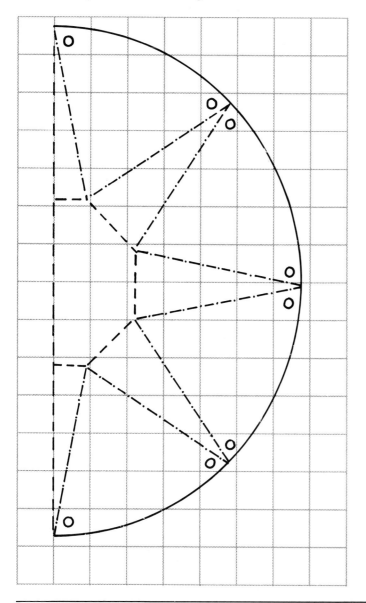

Box with Star [73]

1 Copy the template and transfer it to card as shown. The tabs for glue are not included on the side pieces, so include them at one end. Cut out the shape and score along the fold lines.

2 Fold the box into shape, glue the sides together and fold up the base, gluing it into place.

3 Press the score lines downwards to form a star.

4 The finished box.

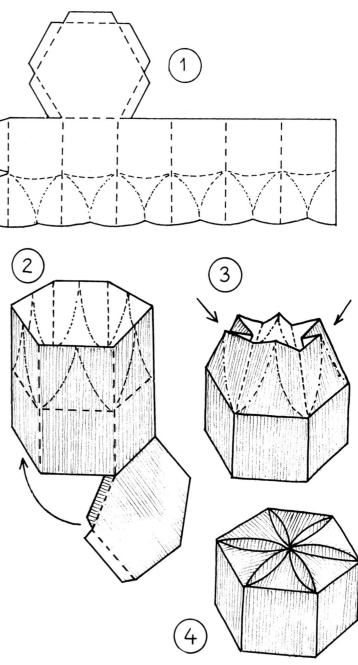

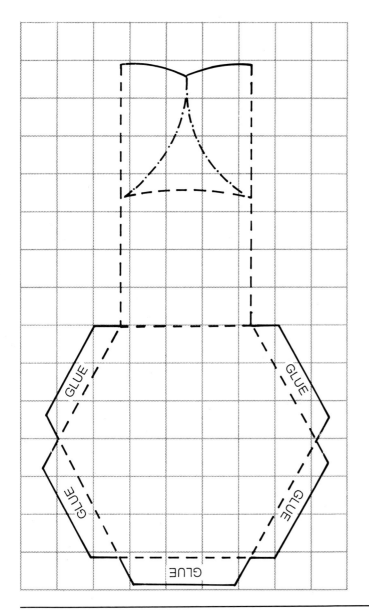

GLUE

Tobacco pouches (page 71); boxes with stars (page 72); pointed boxes (page 75).

Hexagonal Box with Spiral Flaps [65]

1 Transfer the template to card, placing six outlines next to each other as shown. Cut out the shape and score along the fold lines.

2 Glue the sides together.

3 Fold the top by pressing the angles inwards and to the right.

4 Repeat at the bottom.

5 The finished box.

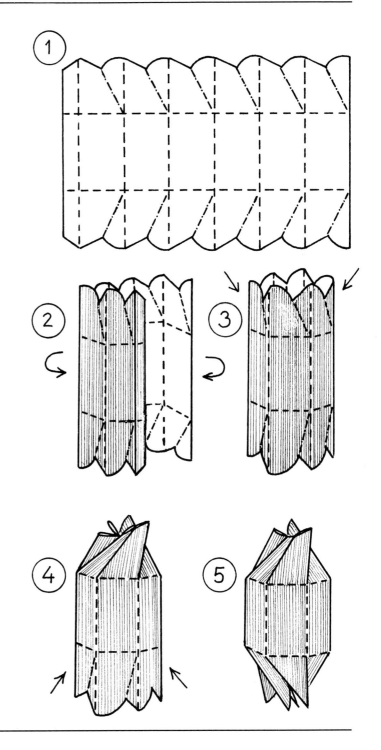

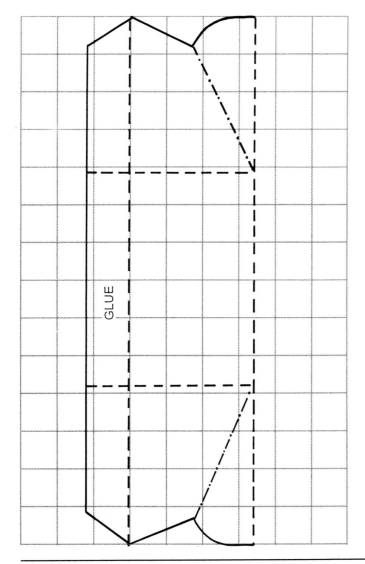

GLUE

Pointed Box [73]

1 Transfer the template to card, placing six outlines next to each other as shown. Cut out the shape and score along the fold lines. Punch the holes.

2 Glue the sides together.

3 Fold the base inwards, tucking the flaps into each other.

4 Fold the curved flaps at the top downwards and inwards to form a point.

5 Thread a piece of cord through the holes.

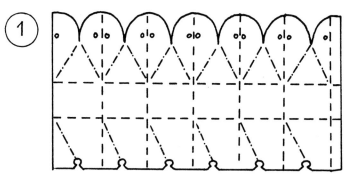

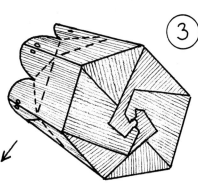

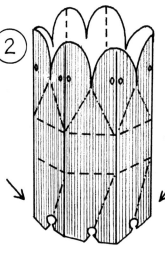

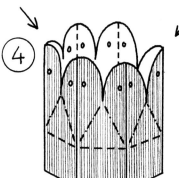

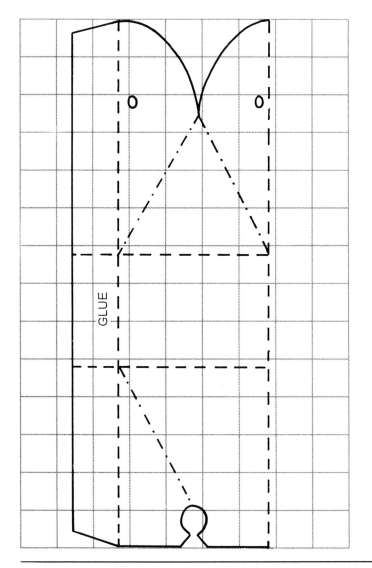

GLUE

O   O

Twin-peaked Triangular Box [57] 🎁 🎁

1 Transfer the template to card, placing two outlines next to each other as shown. Cut out the shape and score along the fold lines.

2 Fold the sides pieces up and inwards as shown.

3 Fold over the ends to form two triangles.

4 Close the box by lifting the triangles to meet in the centre.

5 Tie a piece of ribbon around the box to hold it together.

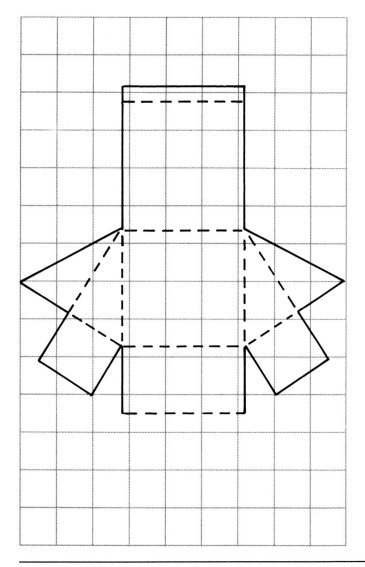

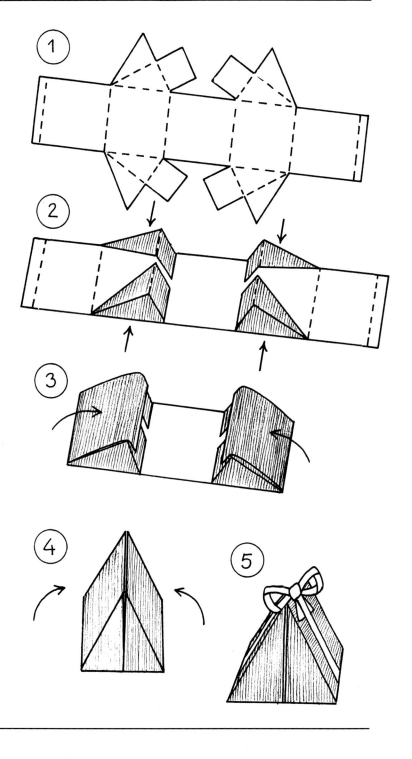